Young Family Parenting Information

Safe Child & Emergencies

Children *cannot* keep themselves safe. Each year many children die or are hurt badly in accidents. Keeping your child safe is a big job. You can prevent many accidents from happening. This book will help you learn how to do this.

Safe Child & Emergencies will also help you to be ready for accidents, so you will know what to do before an accident happens. If your child has an accident, you can give him your best help.

Meld
parenting that works

Developed and Published by

219 North Second Street, Suite 200
Minneapolis, Minnesota 55401
612-332-7563

Staff
Teri Holgate
Victoria Hosch
Mary Nelson
Mary Kay Stranik
Sherry Wendelin

Consultants
Patricia Boris
Katherine Colón
Zardoya Eagles
Elizabeth Verdick

Cover art by Mary Beth Berg

©1987 Meld; 2002 Revised and Updated

ISBN: 0-9676470-7-X

The information in this book is true and complete to the best of our knowledge. This book is intended only as a guide. In no way is this book intended to replace, countermand or conflict with the advice given to you by your doctor or other health care provider. All recommendations are made without guarantees on the part of the authors. The authors and publishers disclaim all liability in connection with the use of this information.

Books in the Young Family Series

Baby Is Here!

Feeding Your Child

Healthy Child/Sick Child

Safe Child & Emergencies

Baby Grows

Baby Plays

The Meld Philosophy

We can learn from each other.

We can support each other.

We can cooperate, yet maintain individuality.

We can make informed decisions.

We, at Meld, believe that parents are experts on their own children. The materials included in this book are intended to provide the best information available. With this as a guide, parents can make good decisions for their individual family's needs. We wish both parents and children joy and success as they grow through this process!

Table of Contents

Chapter 1
Accidents

Why Accidents Happen

Preventing Accidents

The Word	What It Means	Where to Find It
accident	Baby or child getting hurt!	Page 3
childproof	Make and keep an area safe for a baby or small child.	Page 27
poisons	Things that will hurt you if you taste, swallow, smell, or touch them.	Page 34
safety equipment	Things to keep your child safe, or things that help in an emergency.	Page 15

Why Accidents Happen

Accidents happen to many children.

Accidents can hurt or kill children.

Your child *cannot* keep himself safe!

You can help prevent bad accidents from happening.

Children Cannot Keep Themselves Safe

Why not?

- Children *do not* know the difference between "this is safe" and "this is *not* safe."

- Children *do not* know why things happen.

- Children *do not* remember everything.

Here is what a child **cannot** think!

Ball downstairs. Do not get ball. I could fall. I could get hurt!

Here is what a child thinks!

Pretty ball!

Parents Help Prevent Accidents

You and other family members must protect your child.

You must keep your child safe! Your child cannot protect herself.

Protecting your child so that she does not have an accident is very important.

What can you do to keep your child safe?

Watch your child when you are:

- alone with your child
- having visitors
- working in your home
- reading
- watching TV
- shopping
- visiting a friend's home
- at meetings, parties, or clubs
- at your place of worship

Can you think of more times to watch your child?

Keep checking on your child.

Your child may be OK now.

15 minutes later, your child may **not be OK.** Keep checking!

Make the place where you live safe ("childproof").

More about this later. See pages 27–28.

Try to think like your child thinks.

Know what your child will do next.
More about this later. See pages 12–13.

Important!

Your child needs you to keep her safe.

Find out what your child is doing.

Check on your child again and again.

Here are some things you *should not* think about your child and safety:

- "He would not do that."
- "She knows better."
- "I already told him about this."
- "She does not know how to do that yet."
- "He needs to learn his lesson."
- "I told her, no!"
- "He will not think about doing that."

The Most Dangerous Times

Most accidents happen when parents *are not* watching their child closely. Accidents happen when:

- families have many problems on their minds
- problems last a long time (everyone gets worn out)
- families are doing too many things (very busy)
- children are left with other children who are too young
- families are using or abusing drugs and alcohol

Accidents can happen more often in a family when

Child is:

- hungry
- tired or sick
- ignored

Mother is:

- pregnant
- tired or sick
- fighting
- tense (upset, worried)
- in a hurry or very busy
- taking medicine
- using drugs or alcohol

Father is:

- tired or sick
- fighting
- tense (upset, worried)
- in a hurry or very busy
- taking medicine
- using drugs or alcohol

Family or others in home are:

- tired or sick
- fighting
- tense (upset, worried)
- in a hurry or very busy
- using drugs or alcohol

Not OK!

This is when accidents happen most:

- when parents think their child can take care of herself—she *cannot!*
- when there is no safe place for the child to play
- when someone new is taking care of the child
- when a babysitter is too young to take good care of the child
- when a child is in a new place
    - new home
    - vacation
    - daycare
    - friend's home

Does this happen in your family?

Yes?

You can help keep accidents from happening.

Try to:

- Slow down!

- Be more careful!

Important!

Remember that children think like children.

Children cannot think like adults, even if they act like little adults sometimes.

Children want to be like adults. But they are still children.

Young children *cannot* take care of themselves.

Be especially careful when:

- you are drinking alcohol

- you are taking medicines

Can you think of other times that make it hard for you to watch your child closely? *Be more careful at these times.*

How to Slow Down, Relax

Relaxed parents help children to be safer and happier.

When you have stress or feel tense it is hard to watch your child closely.

Accidents can happen at these times!

What can you do if you are worried about many things?

Learn to relax.

This is one way to relax. Try it.

1. Sit or lie down in a calm place. Make yourself comfortable.

2. Stretch out your whole body.

3. Relax your muscles.

4. Breathe slowly. Breathe deeply.

5. Imagine that your arms, hands, legs, and feet feel warm and heavy.

6. Think about something beautiful.
    - A flower.
    - The beach.
    - Your child's smile.
    - Anything that makes you feel calm and happy!

7. Do this as long as you can. It will help you feel more calm and relaxed.

Here are more things to help you relax.

Talk about your problems and worries with:
- family
- friends
- religious leader
- counselor
- parent support group
- health care provider
- any person you trust

Take time for yourself. Do something nice for yourself.
- Take a walk or run.
- Make something for yourself.
- Go out with friends.
- Listen to music.
- Go to the park.

Do you feel mad? Do something that takes a lot of energy.
This will help to get the anger out.

- Walk, run, or exercise.

- Clean your house.

- Build something.

- Cut the grass.

- Cook a meal.

Do something for your family or friends.

- Visit them.

- Write letters to them.

- Make something special for them.

Can you think of more ways to relax?

Important!

- It is OK to cry!
  It is OK for mothers and fathers to cry.
  It is OK to feel bad.

- Mistakes are OK!
  You do not need to be perfect. No one is!
  You do not need to always win.

- Sometimes other people will say you are wrong.
  Decide what you think.
  Try not to worry. Keep doing your best.

- Sometimes you might feel lonely. Visit or call your family or friends.

- Find ways to make new friends:

  - at school or work

  - at meetings or clubs

  - through other friends and family

  - at parent support groups

  - at your place of worship

Can you think of more ways to make new friends?

Be Ready for Your Baby's Changes

A child grows and changes very fast. You need to learn what your child will do next.

Why?

- You can change your actions so accidents are less likely to happen.

- You can change the place where you live so accidents are less likely to happen.

The following chart will help you think about:

- How your baby's actions can cause accidents.

- What you can do to keep your baby safe.

You may find it helpful to talk about these pages with someone and write in the answers.

Important!

A child will copy his parents and family. Your child will try to do what you do and what other people do.

Examples:

- Your baby sees you go downstairs. Your baby wants to go downstairs. But your baby does not know how! Your baby could have an accident!

- Your child sees you shave. Your child wants to try it, too. But this is too dangerous for your child! Your child could get hurt!

Can your baby do this?	What accidents can happen?	What can you do to make things safe for your baby?
Move to the side of the crib		
Grab or hit things		

Can your baby do this?	What accidents can happen?	What can you do to make things safe for your baby?
Put her hands or objects in her mouth		
Roll over		
Sit alone for 1 minute with no help		
Crawl		
Feed himself		
Climb		
Hold furniture to help herself stand		
Hold furniture and walk at the same time		

Preventing Accidents

> **Copy this page. Put it by your phone. If you need to use another person's phone, put this page in a place where you can find it fast. If your baby has an accident, you will need these phone numbers to call for help.**

Important Phone Numbers *(Remember to include area codes.)*

Fire, Police, Community Emergency: **911**

Poison Control Center _____

Doctor's office _____

    Doctor's name _____

    Nurse's name _____

Doctor's office after hours _____

Hospital Emergency Room _____

Your doctor's hospital _____

    Hospital address _____

_____

Friends or family who can help:

Name	Phone Number
_____	_____
_____	_____
_____	_____

Drugstore_____

Taxi _____

Child Abuse Prevention _____

Important!

Do not be afraid to call or go for help if your child needs it. You are **not** a bad parent if your child has an accident. All children have accidents.

Your child is not a bad child because he had an accident. Children do not have an accident to make parents mad or get them in trouble. The most important thing is to get help for your child.

People may ask you questions about the accident. Try to answer any questions as honestly as you can. This will help people to help your child.

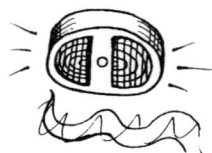

Safety Equipment

It is important to have safety equipment in your house. These items help keep your child safe. Or they help when there is an emergency.

Bring the chart on the following pages to your baby's first checkup at the doctor's office. Ask the doctor or nurse if they know about more safety equipment.

Buy medicine and equipment for your home or borrow some equipment from someone.

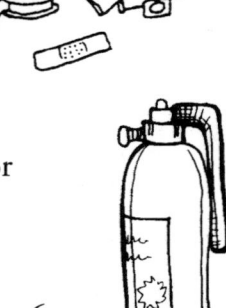

Check the medicine and safety equipment every 6 months. You need to make sure you have enough. You also need to make sure that it is still working.

What to Buy	What Is It For?	Where to Find It
Syrup of Ipecac (Check the expiration date. Make sure it is still good before you use it.)	It makes a child vomit (throw up) if she swallows poison. *Never* give your child this medicine unless your doctor or the Poison Control Center tells you to. It is dangerous to throw up some poisons like bleach.	Drugstore
Smoke alarm	Tells you when there is smoke (maybe fire) in your home. Make sure the batteries are OK. Check them every 6 months!	Discount store Hardware store
Carbon monoxide alarm	Tells you when there are exhaust fumes in your home. These can come from your furnace or fireplace. But you cannot smell them! It is very important to have an alarm. You and your family can die from breathing these fumes.	Discount store Hardware store
Fire extinguisher	Helps you put out small fires.	Discount store Hardware store
Safety latches or locks	Locks cupboards or drawers so that your baby cannot get poisons or things that can hurt her.	Discount store Hardware store Drugstore Children's store

What to Buy	What Is It For?	Where to Find It
Safety plugs for electric outlets	Blocks electric outlet openings so your baby cannot get a shock.	Discount store Hardware store Drugstore Children's store
Safety gate	Keeps your baby from going up or down the stairs, or from going in rooms that are not safe.	Discount store
Bandages Sterile gauze Gauze tape	They keep cuts clean and protected.	Drugstore
Playpen (You do not need this but it is nice to have.)	This is a safe place to put your baby for a short time.	Discount store Children's store Second-hand store
Corner guards (You do not need these but they are nice to have.)	They cover hard edges and corners on furniture to make the edges softer. Your baby will not get hurt as badly if he falls against the edges.	Drugstore Hardware store

Can you think of more safety equipment you might need?

What to Buy	What Is It For?	Where to Find It

What if you do not have money to buy safety equipment?

You may be able to borrow some of these items, like a playpen or safety gate. Ask your family, friends, neighbors, local clinic, or place of worship to lend you what you need.

Hint!

Take a tennis ball. Cut it halfway through. Use as a corner guard for your tables.

Here are some other ideas for safety equipment that you can use:

Instead of:	Use:
Fire extinguisher	Baking soda, flour, corn starch
Safety latches or locks	Rope, a long smooth stick (put the stick through the door handle of your cupboards)
Safety gate	A board without sharp edges (be sure your baby cannot knock it down)

Help the Babysitter to Be Responsible

When you go out, you may want to let your child stay at home. You may ask an older family member (like your mother, brother, sister, uncle, or aunt) to watch your child.

If an adult family member cannot take care of your child, you may ask a young family member (like a cousin, nephew, or niece). Or, you may ask a friend or neighbor to babysit.

No matter who takes care of your child, you want that person to keep your child safe. Make sure you choose someone you can depend on.

Maybe your babysitter has not taken care of young children very much. You can help the sitter to keep your child safe.

How?

- You can show the sitter how to prevent accidents from happening.
- You can tell the sitter what to do if an accident happens.

Who is a good babysitter?

A good babysitter is someone who

- is old enough to watch your baby
- likes children
- pays attention to your baby
- follows your directions
- helps when your baby is in trouble
- has experience with children your baby's age

A good babysitter will also do these things with your child:

- play with your child
    - blocks
    - puppets
    - finger games
    - ball
    - cars
    - dolls
    - puzzles

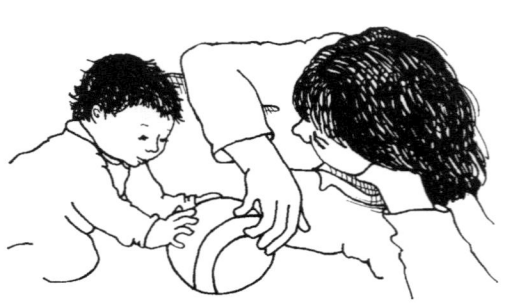

- talk to your child
- be gentle with your child
- feed your child when he is hungry
- put your child to bed when he is tired
- change your child's diapers
- comfort and calm your child
- read stories to your child
- take away dangerous things

What if you disagree with your babysitter?

Is your child's grandmother (or some other older relative) taking care of your child?

Does she do some things that you do not like?

OR

Do you want to tell her about how *you* want her to keep your child safe?

What can you do?

1. Tell her the things that you like about what she does with your child. Then tell her that you do some things a little bit different. Ask her to please do those things the way you do it. Tell her that is what your baby is used to. Show her how to do it.

   OK!

   Example: You want her to hold the baby when she feeds him. You could say, "When you feed the baby, please hold him. He likes it so much when you hold him. He likes to eat this way, and he will not choke." Show her how the baby likes to be held when he eats.

2. Tell her that you are trying some new things to keep your child safe. Show her what you are doing. Ask her to please do it the same way that you do it.

   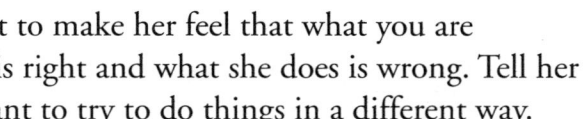

   Not OK!

   Example: You do not want her to hold the baby while she is cooking. You could say, "I am trying something new to keep the baby safe. I do not hold him while I cook at the stove. His clothes could catch fire. So, I put him in a safe place until I am done." Suggest a safe place where she could put the baby while she cooks.

   Try not to make her feel that what you are doing is right and what she does is wrong. Tell her you want to try to do things in a different way.

Also, it may help to talk to other parents. Ask them how they deal with trying to do things in a different way than grandparents, aunts, sisters, or other caregivers.

Where can you find a babysitter?

Ask your friends who have a baby the same age as yours. You can take turns. One time your friend takes care of your baby. One time you take care of hers.

Ask the youth group at your place of worship. They may know older teens (more than 15 years old) who would like to take care of small children.

If you cannot pay a babysitter, maybe you could do something in exchange. You could offer to teach your sitter how to do something like cook, sew, make crafts, or do car repair.

Important!

Babysitting is a serious job. Your babysitter must pay attention to your child and do nothing else while your child is awake. Make sure that your babysitter understands this.

A good babysitter will *not* do things that make it hard to watch your child carefully, like:

- have visitors
- talk on the phone
- watch TV when your child is awake
- do unsafe things like using drugs or alcohol
- leave your child alone in the house

What can you teach the babysitter?

Ask your babysitter to come to your home early.

1. If it is the first time for this babysitter to stay with your child, have her come 1 hour before you go.

   Why?

   - You need to teach her some things:
     - emergency phone numbers
     - the rooms in your home
     - the rules of your home
     - what to say if people call on the phone or stop by
     - how to lock the doors
     - where the baby's clothes are kept
     - how to make the baby's food
     - where the toys are kept

   Can you think of more things to teach the sitter?

   - The babysitter needs time to play with your baby while you are still at home.

     Why?

     - Your baby needs time to get to know a new person.
     - You need to watch how the babysitter plays with your baby.

   - The babysitter needs time to ask questions about your baby.

2. When the babysitter comes again, ask him to come 15 minutes before you go.

   Why?
   Each time the sitter comes, you need to give her:

   • special information from "What My Babysitter Should Know" on pages 25–26

   • time to ask questions about your baby

The next two pages have directions for your babysitter. Before you write on these pages, make several copies to keep at home.

Write in the information that best fits your family. Give it to your babysitter each time.

Hint!

The American Red Cross has a Babysitter's Handbook that is clear and easy to understand. Topics of safety, play, discipline, and first aid are covered very well. You might want to call the Red Cross. Ask them if they have any Babysitter's Handbooks for sale.

What My Babysitter Should Know

Fill out this sheet and give it to your babysitter when you go out. Give the sitter a new sheet every time.

Fire or Police: **911**

Poison Control Center _____

Doctor's office _____

      Doctor's name _____

Doctor's office after hours _____

Mother's name _____

Father's name _____

Home address _____

_____

Home phone number _____

Place mother will be at _____

      Address _____

      Phone _____

      Mother will be back at _____

Place father will be at _____

      Address _____

      Phone _____

      Father will be back at _____

Neighbor

      Name _____

      Address _____

      Phone _____

Other important phone numbers (of family members, friends):

_____

_____

_____

Child's Food

What kind? _____

_____

How much? _____

What time? _____

Where is medicine kept? _____

_____

Other directions about medicine: _____

Bedtime and Naptime

What time? _____

What to do to help baby go to bed: _____

_____

Other directions about bedtime or naptime: _____

_____

Questions or problems you had while I was gone: _____

_____

_____

_____

_____

_____

Childproofing Your Home

You need to "childproof" your home so that your child will be safe.

Your child *cannot* keep himself safe! It is your job to keep your child safe.

Does your baby roll, crawl, walk, or climb?

If he does, he can reach many dangerous things. Make all areas of your home safe for your child.

How can you keep your child safe?

1. Stay near your child.

   Examples:

   - in the bathtub

   - in the car or on the bus

   - in the kitchen

OK!

2. Make and keep each area safe for your baby (childproof).

   Examples:

   - Use a safe car seat in the car or on the bus.

   - Lock medicines in a cabinet or put them up high.

   - Keep garbage locked away.

     Why?
     There are many unsafe things in the garbage:

     – cans

     – plastic

     – glass

     – old food

     – small objects baby may choke on

3. If you *cannot* make an area safe for your child, then keep your child away from that area!

Examples:

- Put a safety gate at all stairs (or put furniture that your child *cannot* move in front of the stairs).

- Close the bathroom door.

  Why? There are many unsafe things in the bathroom.

  – Your child can get burns from hot water.

  – The toilet has germs.

  – Your child could slip and fall.

  – There is water in the bathroom. Your child could drown.

  – There is garbage in the bathroom.

  – There are poisons (like medicines, soap, cleaners, and shampoo) in the bathroom.

  – There are dangerous objects like tweezers and scissors. Your child could get cut.

- Check all tabletops. Remove any object that might hurt your baby or small items she could choke on.

- Watch your baby carefully around furniture that has sharp corners.

- Remove furniture that your baby can tip (unstable chairs, plant stands, wobbly stools).

- Watch your baby near fireplaces! Your baby could get burned. He could bump his head on the hearth. He could touch dangerous fireplace tools.

- Watch your baby very carefully near windows. Make sure they have good screens that *cannot* be pushed out by your child!

- Look for small objects on the floor, like pins and paper clips. Pick them up before your baby does.

> **Hint!**
> Get down on the floor at your baby's eye level. Look at every room from where your baby sees it. You may find things like buttons, pet food, and coins. Pick them up. These things are not safe for babies and young children. They will put them in their mouth and might choke.

Rules for Childproofing the Car

#1	**Drive safely!**

#2	**Do not leave your baby alone in the car—even if you run into the store for a couple of minutes.**

Always take your baby with you.

Why?

- Someone could take your baby.
- The car can get too hot for your baby.
- The car can get too cold for your baby.

Important!

Parents have a lot of things on their mind. Some parents forget that their baby is in the car, especially if the baby is facing toward the back of the car. They leave their baby alone in the car. Babies can die when they are left in the car because it gets too hot or too cold.

Find a way to remember that your baby is in the back seat of the car. Put a clip with your baby's name on it on:

- the visor
- your seat belt
- the top of your baby's car seat

The clip will remind you that your baby is in the car.

#3   Use a safe car seat. (Federally Approved)

Hint!

Driving a car? When you are at a stoplight, check on your child.

Riding the bus? Your baby needs to be in a car seat!

All babies and small children must use safe car seats.

Why do you need a safe car seat?

Many babies who are not in safe car seats die in car accidents. A safe car seat will protect your child if you are in a car accident.

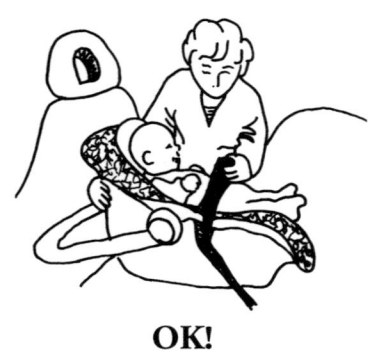

OK!

If your baby is less than
1 year old and less than 20 pounds.

OK!

If your baby is older than 1 year old
and weighs more than 20 pounds.

**#4   Be careful about giving your baby
         snack in the car.**

Don't give snacks to your baby in the car, unless someone is sitting by her and watching her.

If you stop the car suddenly, food could get stuck in her throat. She could choke. Even if you don't stop suddenly, she could start choking and you might not realize it—especially if you can't see her in the rear view mirror.

Rules for Childproofing Against Burns

#1 **Check things that touch your baby. Is it too hot? First, let it cool.**

Why? It is easy to burn your baby!

Check food.

Is it too hot? *Do not* feed it to your baby. Let it cool first.

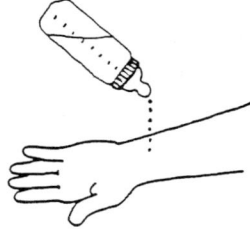

Check bath water.

Is it too hot? *Do not* put your baby in hot water. Add cold water first.

Check the car seat.

Is it too hot? *Do not* put your baby in the seat. Cover the car seat with a blanket or towel first.

Can you think of more things to check?

Not OK!

Is someone eating hot food?

Do not hold the baby.

Why not?
It is easy to spill on the baby. He could get burned by hot foods or drinks.

> ### #2 Keep your baby safe from cooking dangers.

Is someone cooking?

- A hot stove and hot food can burn your baby.

- Put pans on the back burner. Turn pan handles to the middle of the stove.

- Why? Your baby may grab the handles. The hot food might spill on your baby.

- To be safe, keep your baby away from where food is prepared.

Not OK!

Are you cooking?

- *Do not* hold your baby! Why not? Your baby's clothes could catch fire. The hot food could burn your baby.

- *Never* leave your baby alone in the kitchen.

> ### #3 Do not use space heaters.

Why not?
If your baby crawls or walks, she can get close to the heater. She could touch the heater. She could get burned.

Also, **never leave the oven door open for heat.**

> ## #4   Cover radiators.

Your baby may try to touch the radiator.

He *cannot* remember that:

- The radiator is sometimes hot!
- The radiator is sometimes cold!

> ## #5   Cover electric outlets.

Why?

Your baby may put something in an outlet.

Your baby might get a shock or burn.

She could get hurt badly!

> ## #6   Keep dangerous items out of reach.

You need to keep some things where your baby cannot get them. Put them up high where your baby cannot reach. Or put things away in locked drawers or cupboards.

- cigarette lighters
- lit candles
- matches

Rules for Childproofing Against Poisons

Poisons are things that will hurt you if you taste, swallow, smell, or touch them.

> **#1   Lock poisons away from your baby.**

Why?
Your baby will put poisons in his mouth.
He could get very sick.
Your baby could die.

Important!
Do not call medicine "candy." If you do, your child will want to eat lots of medicine when she is not sick.

What things are poisonous to your child?

- medicines
- cleansers
- cigarettes, ashtrays
- animal and insect poisons
- small batteries (like flashlight or toy batteries)
- gasoline, paint, paint thinner
- drugs or alcohol
- nail polish, makeup, and other cosmetics

Can you think of more poisons?

> ## #2   Use good locks on cabinets and drawers.

- "children's safety locks"
  (there are many kinds)
- padlock
- place on high shelf out of
  child's reach

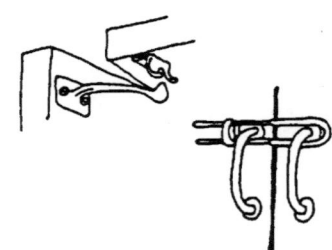

> ## #3   *Never* let your baby suck or eat any part of a plant.

Why not?
Many plants are poisonous. Babies like to eat plants.
Your baby could get sick.

- Put plants up high—away from your child.
- Keep your baby away from plants when outside.

Do you want to know which
plants are poisonous?

Call the Poison Control Center
or Department of Health. They
will tell you.

| #4 | **Know the dangers of lead-based paint.** |

Lead-based paint is a serious health risk.

Why?

Lead is poisonous.

- Babies like to chew on things.
- Paint pieces can get in your baby's mouth.
- Paint with lead in it will make your baby very sick.
- It can hurt your baby's brain.

How can you know if there is lead in the paint?

Look at the label on the paint can.
Is the date after 1978? If yes, the paint is OK!

**If something was painted before 1978, the paint is *not OK!*
Do not let your baby chew it!**

Take any old cans of paint to the recycling center. Keep your baby away from all paint cans!

Important!

Put the Poison Control Center phone number near your phone. Or, put it in a place where you can find it fast.

What if you don't have the paint cans to check the date?

Take some paint chips from your house to the Department of Health. They can test the paint chips to see if there is any lead.

Here are some things that are painted. Babies like to chew on these things. Be sure to check them for lead-based paint.

- crib bars
- window sills
- toys
- furniture
- chips of paint falling from walls, doors, windows, or ceiling

Hint!

For more information on how to keep your baby safe, see "Keeping Your Baby Safe" in the Young Family Parenting Information Book, *Baby Is Here!*

Can you think of more things to check?

#5 Make sure your furnace is safe.

A furnace that is old or not working right can be very dangerous. It can leak carbon monoxide into your home.

Carbon monoxide has no odor.
You cannot smell it.
But it can kill you!

Important!

Keep the basement door closed at all times. Keep baby away from the furnace, tools, and other household dangers.

If your furnace is old or not working right, you need to have somebody check it.

Call the gas company to ask how to get your furnace checked.

Rules for Childproofing Against Choking

#1 Do not leave small things where your child can reach them.

Why not?
Your baby will put them in her mouth. She will choke.
She may not be able to breathe.

- rubber bands
- buttons
- safety pins
- tacks
- hair pins
- pins
- coins
- string
- paper clips

Can you think of more small things?

Make and keep each area safe for your baby.

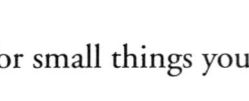

- Get down on the floor and look at it like your baby sees it. Pick up any small objects that might hurt your baby before you put the baby on the floor.
- Check tables, counters, and drawers for small things your baby could find.
- Check under and behind things (like furniture).
- Pick up small things.
- Sweep or vacuum the floor every day.

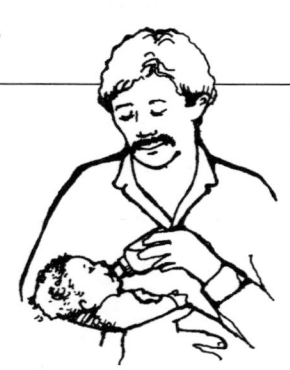

#2 **Hold your baby to feed her.**

If your baby is *not* held, she could:

- choke

- get an ear infection

#3 **Do not give your child foods that can make him choke.**

These foods are **Not OK!**

- nuts

- popcorn

- hot dog slices

- tortilla chips

- whole grapes

- peanut butter on a spoon

- raw carrots

Why are some foods dangerous?

- Grapes, small slices of hot dog, and nuts are round. They can get caught in your baby's throat. Your baby might not be able to breathe. Cut these foods into pieces that will not get caught in your baby's throat.

Hint!

You can cook some foods to make them safe for your baby.

Example:

Your baby might choke on raw carrots. But if you cook the carrots, they turn soft. Let them cool and your baby can eat them safely, if they are not cut round.

- Tortilla chips and popcorn kernels have sharp edges. They might poke and hurt your baby's throat. Babies need softer foods.

- Peanut butter is sticky and might stick in your baby's throat. It might make your baby choke. Some babies are also allergic to peanut butter.

Many foods must be cut up into small pieces for a young child to eat.

Important!

Some foods also cause allergies in small children. Until your baby is 1 year old, don't give him any:

- wheat
- nuts (or peanut butter)
- citrus
- egg whites
- honey
- shellfish (like shrimp or crab)
- berries

#4   Keep all cords away from your child.

Why?

Cords, ropes, and strings can wrap around your baby's neck.

Your baby can choke. Your baby might die.

- Keep phone cords up high and out of reach.

- Do not put necklaces or bracelets on your baby.

- Do not put cords, ribbons, or strings on your baby's pacifier.

- Mobiles or toys with pull cords:

    - Use only toys with short cords.

    - Watch your baby while she plays.

    - Put the toy away when your baby is done playing.

    - Do not leave baby with toys that have strings or cords.

Not OK!

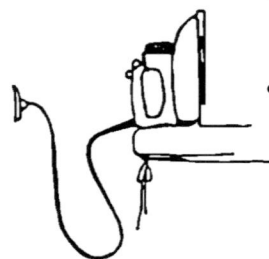

Not OK!

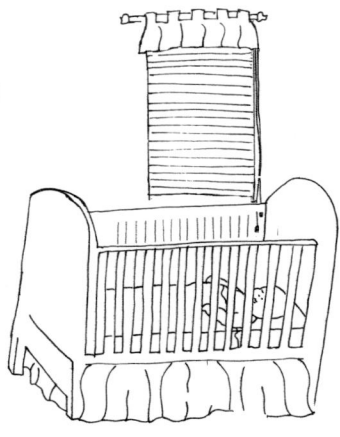

– Take mobiles and toys with pull cords out of your baby's bed when he can sit up by himself.

• Tie curtain cords up high and out of reach.

• Do not have mini blind cords near your baby's crib or within his reach.

• Never leave the iron cord plugged in.

Your baby might pull the iron down. Or it could fall on her by accident.

She could get burned! She could get hurt!

She could choke on the cord.

Not OK!

#5 **Make sure there are no plastic bags near your child.**

Throw them away or keep them in a safe place.

Why?
The plastic could get on your child's face.
She will not be able to breathe.

Your child may want to chew on plastic.
Plastic pieces might get caught in her throat.
She might choke.

• plastic bags from the supermarket

• balloons

• plastic packages

• garbage bags

• plastic wrap for food

Rules for Childproofing Against Bathtub Dangers

#1   Always watch your baby in the bathtub.

Do not take your eyes off your baby even for a minute.

If the phone or doorbell rings, ignore it while you bathe your baby. Your baby could drown if left alone—even if there is only an inch of water.

Important!

Keep doors to bathrooms closed at all times. Bathrooms are not safe places for babies to play or explore.

Do not leave anyone who is less than 12 years old to watch your baby in the tub. Babies are very slippery when wet. An older child might not be able to hold your baby tightly. Your baby could get very hurt. Your baby might drown.

Make sure the water in the bathtub is not too hot before you put the baby in. Make sure your water heater is not turned up too high.

OK!

Not OK!
Your baby can drown
even in a little bit of water.

Rules for Childproofing Against Cuts, Falls, and Injury

> **#1** **Do not keep sharp objects near your baby.**

Why not?
Your baby will try to grab them. He could get hurt.

- clothes hangers
- hair pins
- tacks
- pins
- safety pins
- razors
- knives
- scissors
- pencils

Can you think of more sharp things?

Not OK!

> **#2** **Cover sharp edges on furniture and other things in your home (especially when your child is learning to walk).**

Why?

When children learn to walk, they fall.

Your child could fall. She could hit the edge of the furniture or fireplace. She could get hurt.

Place corner protectors on furniture like coffee tables, end tables, and chairs. These protectors will help prevent injury if your child falls or bumps into them.

> **#3** **Do not use a tablecloth until your child is 3 years old.**

Why not?

Your child will want to pull on the tablecloth.

Things on table will fall on him. He could get hurt or burned.

Your child will pull on the tablecloth to:

- feel the cloth

- get help to stand

- see what is on top of table

> ## #4   Put a safety gate in front of all stairs.

Why?

Your baby can fall down the stairs.

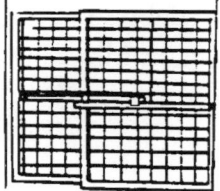

- Put a gate at the top and bottom of stairs.

- Keep the basement door closed.

> ## #5   Protect your baby from falling from high places.

Never leave your baby in a high place.

Do not leave your baby when you answer the phone or the door.

Take him with you.

What if you forget something that you need when you are changing the baby?

Take your baby with you to get it. Do not leave your baby alone on the diaper changing table, even if there is a strap or belt for your baby.

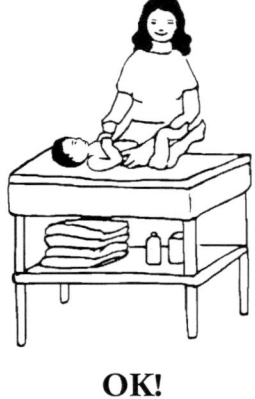

OK!

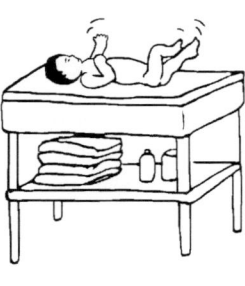

Not OK!

#6　Always watch your baby.

Babies like to climb! If your baby is climbing, she could fall.

#7　*Never shake your baby or play rough.*

Why not?

- Your baby could get hurt.
- Your baby could fall.
- It can hurt your baby's brain very badly if you shake or throw your baby in the air.
- You could also make your baby sick.

Important!

Always call the clinic or doctor's office if:

- someone shakes your baby
- your baby falls and hits his head

Your baby can look OK and then get sick later. The people at the clinic will tell you how to take care of your baby if he falls or if he is shaken.

Rules for Childproofing the Crib

Each year, in the United States, 150 to 200 children *die* because of unsafe cribs. Each year 40,000 babies are *hurt badly* because of unsafe cribs.

> **#1** **Use a crib with bars close together.**

Why?

This keeps your baby safe.

crib bars

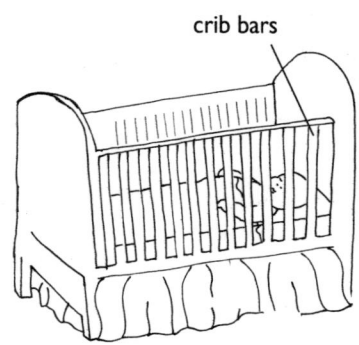

The bars of the crib should be no more than 3 fingers (2 3/8 inches) apart. That way, your baby's arms, legs, and head cannot get caught between the bars.

She could get stuck.
She could stop breathing.
She could choke or get hurt.

OK!

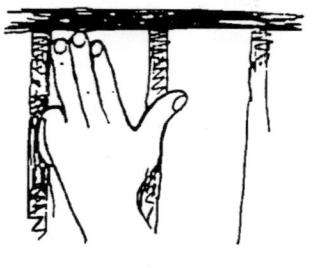

Not OK!

> ## #2 The mattress must fit tight against the crib bars.

If you can fit more than 2 fingers between the mattress and the side of the crib, the mattress is too small. Your baby might get caught between the mattress and the crib bars. Lower the mattress when your baby can stand.

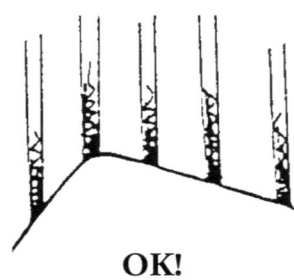

OK!

> ## #3 All parts of the crib must be smooth.

Why?

Your baby could get cuts or splinters.

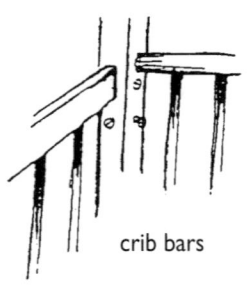

crib bars

No screws, bolts, or
nails can stick

screw or nail

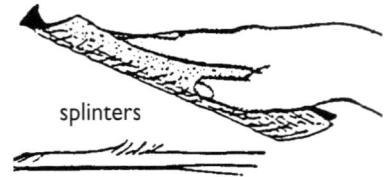

splinters

No rough spots.
Use sandpaper to smooth
the wood of the crib.

> **#4**   **No corner posts on the crib.**

Why not?

Your baby's clothes might get caught on the corner posts and she could get hurt.

> **#5**   **No cutouts in the head board or foot board.**

Why not?

Your baby's head might get caught in the cutout.

> **#6**   ***Do not* put baby to sleep on soft bedding.**

- no waterbeds
- no pillows
- no soft, thick blankets or comforters

These are dangerous. Your baby's face can get smothered in soft bedding. He will not be able to breathe. He could die or get brain damage.

#7 **Do not place pillows or large stuffed animals in the crib.**

Why not?

Your child could stand on these. She may fall out of the crib. She could get hurt.

Pillows or stuffed animals could cover your baby's nose and mouth. She might not be able to breathe.

#8 **Make the crib safe.**

Can your child climb out of the crib?

Lower the mattress so your child cannot climb out.

Not OK!
The mattress is too high for
a child who climbs.

> **#9**   **Your child should not be able to open the crib locks and lower the side of the crib.**

Why not?

Your child could fall out of the crib. Your child could pinch her fingers.

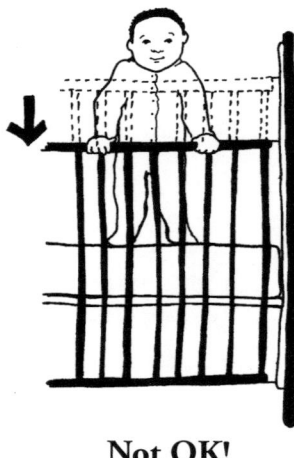

Not OK!

Can your child push the side of the crib down?

Are the locks and sides easy to move?
The crib is not safe!
You need to get a different crib.

> **Hint!**
>
> No crib for your baby? See Young Family Parenting Information, *Baby Is Here!* for ideas about making other places safe for your baby to sleep.

Rules for Childproofing Other Equipment

#1   Use a safe high chair.

What is a safe high chair?

- A safe high chair is *not* easy to tip over.
- A safe high chair has a safety belt or strap.
- A safe high chair does not have wheels.

seat belt

When your child is in the high chair, *do not leave the room*! You need to be able to see your child.

Children are fast. If you are not watching, your child could try to climb out of the chair. He could fall and get hurt.

#2   Use a safe playpen.

Do you have a wooden playpen? Use the same rules as for the crib on page 47–48.

Do you have a playpen with fabric mesh on the sides? If the mesh tears, do not use the playpen.

Why?

Your child could get stuck in the netting and choke. Or, your child could escape from the playpen.

Rules for Childproofing Toys

#1 Buy and make sturdy toys.

Buy or make toys that will not fall apart or break.

Why?

Children like to do these things with their toys:

- throw
- chew
- drop
- pull
- twist
- bend
- bang together
- try to break

Does your child do this to make you mad? No!

Your child needs to play this way.

She is learning important things when she does this.

#2 Check all toys.

Check the toys you have at home.

Check the toys people give to your child.

Why?

Some toys:

- break easily
- have small pieces a child could choke on
- have rough places (use sandpaper to smooth wooden toys)
- have sharp edges or parts

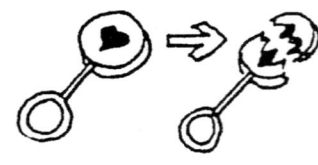

Balloons are especially bad. They can burst into your child's throat and hurt him.

Did you find any of these things?

Do not give the toy to your baby. Fix it or throw it away.

#3   Do not use electric toys.

Why not?

Your child could choke on the cord or get burned.

Your child could get an electric shock from the outlet.

#4   Do not give toys with batteries to your baby.

Why not?

Your child may open the place where the batteries are stored.

He may chew on the batteries and get a bad burn from battery acid.

> **#5   Do not use a toy box with a lid or cover!**

Why not?

The lid could fall on your baby's head or hands.

Your child could be hurt badly.

Your child could climb in the box and get trapped inside.

Where can you put toys?

- in a cardboard box

- in a laundry basket

- in a toy box without a lid or cover

- on a low shelf

Why not on a high shelf?

Your baby may climb to get the toys, and then fall.

Your baby may pull the toys down and hit her head with a toy.

Your baby may climb and tip the shelves over on top of herself.

You do a lot to keep your child safe!

You know what causes accidents.

You know that your baby changes. When she changes, you can do new things to keep her safe.

You childproof your home and car.

You help babysitters to be responsible.

All of these things take a lot of your time. But you know baby's safety is the most important thing.

You should be proud!

Chapter 2
When Accidents Happen

What to Know First

Taking Care of an Injury/Accident

You Are Learning How to Help Your Child

The Word	What It Means	Where to Find It
First Aid	Ways to help a hurt person before you get medical help.	Page 64

What to Know First

There are 3 rules for an emergency:

- **Stay calm.**

- **Get help if you need it.**

- **Keep your child calm.**

If you follow these rules, you can take better care of your child in an emergency.

#1   Stay calm.

Try to look calm, not scared.

How?

Read this chapter. Learn what to do.

Have supplies and equipment in your home for emergencies.

#2   Get help if you need it.

How?

Always have emergency numbers near your phone.

Or, put them in a place where you and the babysitter can find them.

When you call for help, slowly tell what happened.

Tell where you are.

Keep your own address and phone number by your phone for people who might need to call for help:

- the babysitter
- grandparents
- neighbors
- older children

#3   Keep your child calm.

How?

Hold your child.

Use a soothing tone of voice.

Explain to your child what you will do.

Deciding Whom to Call

Different emergencies need different people to help. This list will help you know who to call.

The Problem

Your child:

- chokes, cannot breathe

- is turning blue in the lips or skin

- is bleeding and you cannot stop the blood flow

- is unconscious ("knocked out" or you cannot wake the child up)

What to Do

1. **Call 911**

   The 911 operator will call the ambulance and tell you what to do until they come.

2. Take your child to the emergency room.
   Do not go to the doctor's office.

These are very serious problems. A doctor *cannot* help you in his office. The doctor may need to use the special equipment that is at the hospital.

The Problem

Your child:

- has a burn and a big piece of flesh comes off

- breaks a bone

- has a seizure

  - body shakes a lot

  - cannot control body

  - then, body gets stiff

  - maybe blue skin

- has big cut, needs stitches

Important!

Are you calling an emergency phone number?

Slowly tell them about the problem. Tell them:

- the kind of emergency

- the address and phone number of the emergency

- your name

Your home address and phone number.

What to Do

1. **Call 911**

   The 911 operator will call the ambulance and tell you what to do until they come.

2. Take your child to the emergency room.

These are very serious problems. These problems will not get better without medical help.

The Problem

Your child:

- has put poison in his mouth

- gets poison in his eyes or on his skin

What is a poison? See page 34.

Important!

Do not give your child Syrup of Ipecac until the Poison Control Center or clinic tells you to. Syrup of Ipecac will make your child throw up. It is dangerous to throw up some poisons like bleach. They will burn your child's throat.

What to Do

Call the Poison Control Center.

No Poison Control Center where you live?
Call the clinic, the doctor's office, or the emergency room.

Poisoning is a serious emergency.

The Poison Control Center or clinic will tell you:

- what to do

- what *not* to do

The Problem

Your child:

- has a medium or small size burn

- has had a bad fall or hit her head

- has a sudden change in behavior (it may be from poison, pain, or an injury)

- gets a small deep wound or cut (called a puncture wound)
  Example: Stepping on a nail

What to Do

Call the doctor's office or clinic.

These problems are serious and probably need medical attention.
You need to call a doctor or nurse for advice.

Taking Care of an Injury/Accident

> **When your child has an accident or gets hurt, you can use First Aid.**
>
> **First Aid is a way to help a hurt person, before help comes.**

Sometimes First Aid is all your child needs. Sometimes you need to use First Aid and call the doctor or hospital, too.

These pages will tell you:

- when First Aid is all your child needs
- how to use some simple First Aid

These pages also will tell you when to:

- call your doctor's office or clinic
- go to the emergency room
- call 911
- call the Poison Control Center

First Aid for Choking or Not Breathing

Type of Injury/Accident	What should you do?
Your child drinks or eats too fast. She is choking, but can still breathe.	Most times, you do not need to help your child. She will cough, but she will be OK.
Your child gets her face in some water while taking a bath or swimming. She is choking and coughing.	Take your child out of the water. Does your child feel afraid? Hold her. Talk to her. Help comfort her. This can be scary for you and your child, but it is *not* serious. Try to help your child feel comfortable in the water again.
Your child is choking on food, a toy, or another object. The coughing does *not* stop the choking.	1. Make your child's body straight. 2. Look in your child's mouth. If you see the object and can reach it with your fingers, remove the object. **Be careful! Do not push it down more!** 3. **If the choking does not stop, call 911. CALL RIGHT AWAY!** *continued*

First Aid for Choking or Not Breathing

Type of Injury/Accident	What should you do?
Your child cannot breathe. You may not know why. His skin or his lips may become blue.	1. Look in your child's mouth and throat. Is there some food, a toy, or an object there? 2. If you see the object and can reach it with your fingers, remove the object. **Be careful! Do not push it down more!** **If you are not able to remove the object:** 3. Turn your baby flat on his tummy over your arm, supporting his head in your hand. Pat him hard on his back several times. 4. Look in his mouth again. If you see the object and can reach it with your fingers, remove the object. 5. If you do not see anything in his mouth, repeat Steps 3 and 4. Repeat these steps for only 1 minute. 6. **Call 911 or have someone else call 911. CALL RIGHT AWAY!**

First Aid for Poisoning

Type of Injury/Accident	What should you do?
Your child gets poison in her mouth. What is poison? (See page 34.)	**If your child gets poison in her mouth:** 1. Find the source of the poison. 2. Try to find out how much poison your child put in her mouth: How many pills are gone? (Example: 1 pill, 2 pills, 10 pills) How much liquid is gone? (Example: 1/2 cup, 2 ounces, about a capful) 3. Take the poison source to the phone. **4. Call the Poison Control Center.** If there is no Poison Control Center, call your clinic, doctor's office, or the emergency room. You will need to tell them: • the name of the poison (Read it from the bottle or box.) • how much is gone and how much you think got in your child's mouth • when your child took the poison • how much your child weighs 5. The Poison Control Center, doctor, or emergency room will tell you if you should give your child Syrup of Ipecac. This is medicine to make a person throw up a poison. Sometimes the Poison Control Center or doctor will say yes, sometimes no. *Do not* decide by yourself.

First Aid for Poisoning *(continued)*

Type of Injury/Accident	What should you do?

Your child gets poison in his eyes or on his skin.
 	
What is poison? (See page 34.)
	If your child gets poison in his eyes or on his skin:
	
	1. Find the source of the poison.
	
	2. Flush your child's eyes or skin with lots and lots of clean water.
	
	3. Call the Poison Control Center.
	
	If there is no Poison Control Center, call your clinic, doctor's office, or the emergency room. You will need to tell them:
	
	  • the name of the poison (Read it from the bottle or box.)
	
	  • how much is gone and how much you think got in your child's eyes or on his skin
	
	4. The Poison Control Center, doctor, or emergency room will tell you what you need to do next.

Hint!

Look up the number for the Poison Control Center and keep it close to the telephone.

First Aid for Burns

Your child might get a burn. How?

- Something hot touches your child. (Example: hot water, hot food)

- Your child gets too close to something hot. (Example: stove, oven, heater)

- Your child touches electricity. (Example: puts something in an electrical outlet)

Type of Injury/Accident	What should you do?
1st degree burns (burns that turn red but do not blister)	1. Take off your child's clothes so that you can see the burn. 2. Put the burned area in a sink of clean, cold water for no more than 10 minutes. 3. Later, if the burn hurts again, put a clean, cold, wet washcloth on the burn. 4. Does the burn still hurt? Call the doctor's off or clinic.
2nd degree burns (burns that blister)	1. Take off your child's clothes so that you can see the burn. 2. Put the burned area in a sink of clean, cold water for no more than 10 minutes. 3. Cover the burn with a clean, dry cloth. *Do not* put medicine or anything else on the cloth or burn. 4. **Your child should be seen by a doctor.**

Important!
Do not put a cold pack on the burn. It can freeze your baby's skin and hurt it.

First Aid for Burns *(continued)*

Type of Injury/Accident	What should you do?
3rd degree burns (skin may look white, brown, or charred)	1. Put the burned area in a sink of clean, cool water. Or, pour clean, cool water over the burned area. 2. Place a clean, dry cloth around the burn. *Do not* put water, medicine, or anything else on the cloth or burn.  2. **Take your child to the emergency room right away or call 911.**

Important!

Do not put these things on burns. They can make the burn worse.

- antiseptic spray
- butter
- oil
- baking soda

Do *not* open a blister or take off burnt skin.

First Aid for Wounds on the Skin

Type of Injury/Accident	What should you do?
Splinters	Soak the splinter in warm, soapy water before trying to remove it.
	• Soapy water cleans the wound and makes the skin soft.
	• Water makes the splinter swell up. This makes it easier to get the splinter out.
Cuts, scratches, bites, and puncture wounds cut scratch	1. Wash the skin with soap and warm water. Get the dirt off and clean the wound area. 2. The wound must be soaked 3 times for 10 minutes each time. (Washing the wound will clean out the dirt and germs.) Use warm, *clean* water and soap *each* time. 3. If the wound bleeds after washing it, hold it tight or apply pressure to it for 3 to 4 minutes using a clean cloth, bandage, or diaper. Keep the wound pointing up not down. This will help the bleeding to stop. If the wound still bleeds, hold it tight for another 3 to 4 minutes. *continued*

First Aid for Wounds on the Skin

Type of Injury/Accident	What should you do?
Cuts, scratches, bites, and puncture wounds bite puncture	**4.** When the bleeding stops, look at the wound. Take your child to the doctor if: • the cut is big and open • it needs stitches • the cut is on your child's face • you cannot tell if the cut or wound is bad or not • the wound keeps on bleeding **5.** If the wound does not need stitches, put antibiotic ointment on the wound and cover with a loose bandage. When possible, leave the bandage off. Air helps heal the skin. **6.** Call the doctor's office or clinic if your child has a: • puncture wound (A puncture wound can be very dangerous, especially if it does not bleed.) • bite (from an animal or a person) • very dirty wound The doctor will decide if your child needs: • a tetanus booster shot • antibiotic medicine **7.** Watch how the wound heals. Call the doctor's office or clinic if the wound: • gets red • has pus • gets swollen • is hot • keeps hurting The wound might have an infection.

First Aid for Falls

Type of Injury/Accident	What should you do?
Your child has fallen hard and is crying. You wonder how badly she is hurt.	1. Do not move her right away. 2. Look at your child's whole body. **Look for broken bones:** • A bone may be in the wrong place. • A bone may be sticking our of the skin. • Some broken bones are hard to see. How will you know if a bone is broken? • Ask your child to move the part of her body that hurts. if a bone is broken, the hurt part will *not* move. • If your child is too young to understand, watch your child move. Can she use the hurt part of her body like she did before the accident? • If she *cannot* move the hurt part, she may have a broken bone or a bad injury. **Your child needs to see a doctor right away if:** • you can see a broken bone • your child *cannot* move the hurt part of her body • your child *cannot* walk or crawl well *continued*

First Aid for Falls

Type of Injury/Accident	What should you do?
	Check to see if he hit his head.
	How will you know?
	There may be a cut, bump, or bruise on his head.
	Your child may:
	• be sleepy (wants to sleep, not alert)
	• vomit (throw up)
	• be dizzy
	• say things that don't make sense
	• have trouble seeing
	The pupils (black dots) in the middle of your child's eyes may get very big or one may be bigger than the other.
	Your child's behavior may change. He may act differently than usual.
	Your child might have blood coming from his ears or mouth.
	If your child has any of these signs, he may have a head injury. Your child needs to see a doctor right away.

Important!

Sometimes children are very upset after a fall. This may make a child vomit (throw up) or want to sleep, even if his head is not injured. Call your doctor if you are not sure whether your child is hurt or just very upset.

Ways to Learn More about First Aid

First Aid is very important!

These pages have told you about only a few injuries. They have told you about only the most simple ways to help your child.

There is much more to learn!

How can you learn more?

1. Take a class that teaches parents about First Aid and emergency care for babies and children.

    Here are some places to look for classes:
    *   the Red Cross
    *   your doctor's office or clinic
    *   the Department of Health
    *   your friends and family

2. Read books about First Aid and emergency care.

    One good book is: *A Sigh of Relief,* by Martin I. Green, published by Bantam Books.

    This book has fast, easy ways to take care of a child's injury.

    It has many pictures to show you what to do.

    Another good book is: *Babysitter's Handbook,* published by the American Red Cross.

You Are Learning How to Help Your Child

You do a lot to help when your child has an accident.

You know who to call for help.

You have important phone numbers by your phone or in a place that is easy to find.

You have important supplies in your home.

You know how to help your child using First Aid.

You can learn more about First Aid and emergencies.

All people are worried and afraid when their child has an accident. But you are learning how to help your child.

You should be proud!

Meld
parenting that works

Order Form

Qty.	Title	$ Each	Total
	Complete Six-Book Set **SAVE!**	$60.00	
	Baby Is Here!	$12.00	
	Feeding Your Child	$12.00	
	Healthy Child/Sick Child	$12.00	
	Safe Child & Emergencies	$12.00	
	Baby Grows	$12.00	
	Baby Plays	$12.00	

Subtotal _____

Shipping & handling _____

MN residents add 6.5% sales tax* _____

Total _____

*Tax exempt #: _____

Shipping & Handling

For orders subtotaling:

Up to $25	$5.00
$25.01 to $75	$7.00
$75.01 to $150	$9.00
Over $150	8% of subtotal

Please call for Air Delivery Services and International Delivery pricing.

All orders must be prepaid.

Most orders are shipped within 2 days from receipt of order (7 to 9 delivery days).

Call for quantity discounts!

Send book(s) to:

Name _____

Agency _____

Street address _____

City _____

State _____ Zip _____

Telephone _____

Email _____

Method of Payment:

☐ Check or money order payable to Meld

☐ Visa   ☐ MasterCard   ☐ American Express

Account No. _____

Exp. Date _____

Signature _____

Mail to:
Meld • 219 North Second Street • Suite 200
Minneapolis, MN 55401

You can also order by phone, fax or on our website!

612-332-7563   612-344-1959 (fax)   www.meld.org

Meld
parenting that works

Order Form

Qty.	Title	$ Each	Total
	Complete Six-Book Set **SAVE!**	$60.00	
	Baby Is Here!	$12.00	
	Feeding Your Child	$12.00	
	Healthy Child/Sick Child	$12.00	
	Safe Child & Emergencies	$12.00	
	Baby Grows	$12.00	
	Baby Plays	$12.00	

Subtotal _____

Shipping & handling _____

MN residents add 6.5% sales tax* _____

Total _____

*Tax exempt #: _____

Shipping & Handling

For orders subtotaling:

Up to $25	$5.00
$25.01 to $75	$7.00
$75.01 to $150	$9.00
Over $150	8% of subtotal

Please call for Air Delivery Services and International Delivery pricing.

All orders must be prepaid.

Most orders are shipped within 2 days from receipt of order (7 to 9 delivery days).

Call for quantity discounts!

Send book(s) to:

Name _____

Agency _____

Street address _____

City _____

State _____ Zip _____

Telephone _____

Email _____

Method of Payment:

☐ Check or money order payable to Meld

☐ Visa   ☐ MasterCard   ☐ American Express

Account No. _____

Exp. Date _____

Signature _____

Mail to:
Meld • 219 North Second Street • Suite 200
Minneapolis, MN 55401

You can also order by phone, fax or on our website!

612-332-7563   612-344-1959 (fax)   www.meld.org